Creating FAMILY Traditions

Creating FAMILY Traditions

Building Lasting Love and Values

Jeanne Yawney

Second Printing: August 1996

International Standard Book Number:
0-88290-525-2

Horizon Publishers' Catalog and Order Number
1054

Printed and distributed
in the United States of America by

Horizon
Publishers
& Distributors, Incorporated
P.O. Box 490 Bountiful, Utah 84011-0490

Contents

Jeanne and her Family
Front row: Mark, Davis, Jill. *Back row:* Matt, Jeanne, David.
Not shown: Jeremy (out of the country when photo was taken).

About the Author

Jeanne Yawney taught school for three years before choosing a career in the creative art of professional homemaking and motherhood. Although she loved the school children and the many varied aspects of teaching, her "career change" has been anything but mundane. She reads nutrition books and cookbooks the way other people read novels. She also grows and preserves nearly all of her family's fruits and vegetables. Her love for dried flowers blossomed into a home business.

Jeanne's motto is, "If you want to enjoy your work more, work harder!" Because home and family have been her life's work, she has made it more rewarding by constantly finding and creating ideas to make home life more fun. She has also shared her talents through extensive church activity, serving as both a teacher and in the leadership of various organizations.

Jeanne grew up on a farm in Fleming, Saskatchewan, Canada, in a family of eight children. She obtained her teaching certificate from the University of Regina. Jeanne and her husband, David, live in Raymond, Alberta, Canada. They are the parents of five children.

1
Family Bonding

If I were to ask you the high points of your childhood, could you name the exact places they happened and how old you were when they occured? I can. My favorite memories were "in the kitchen, at about 3:30 and 7:00 p.m., ages six through seventeen." That's right, my favorite memories happened almost every day.

For example, I'll always remember the informal family lunches we had each day after school when I was younger. The whole family would gather around the table to enjoy mom's homemade bread and jam while we shared the news of the day. I always felt loved and important when the whole family seemed interested in what I had to say.

A daily high from my teenage years, believe it or not, was doing the nightly dishes with my mom or sister. Depending on the night, our conversations ranged from the trivial to the sharing of our deepest feelings. Some nights we would end up crying and hugging each other, and other nights we would laugh so hard we couldn't breathe!

The Habit of Having Fun Together

My favorite memories happened almost every day because *my family was in the habit of doing things together.* I believe my family's habits and traditions created an environment in which we were creative and spontaneous with one another. Those ordinary times, mixed with the right amount of variety, helped make for a close, family life. We had a tradition of having fun together.

I promise you that these kinds of childhood memories are more than remnants of a less-hurried era gone by. You may not believe it but it's true: families can still spend quality time together, even in our fast-paced society. You just need to choose your family traditions carefully.

Consider how many traditions your family already has. I'm not only talking about how you spend Christmas together, but how you eat together, what you do before bed, what you do after church every Sunday. You probably have a routine for these times already; the challenge is to create patterns or traditions that make the most of these times, turning them into bonding moments.

Start With the Most Important Habits

If you have daily family prayer and scripture study and weekly Family Home Evenings, you know that these activities make a big difference. If you're not doing all of them, I would recommend putting them into place right away! The most important tradition you can have is to be obedient to these commandments and invite the Spirit into your home daily.

I wrote this book because the Lord has told us that more than ever, children need strong family ties to survive in this increasingly wicked and confusing world. When our children's needs for "connecting" are not met in the home, they may look elsewhere to have those needs met. To prevent them from going elsewhere, parents need to help children feel safe and protected in their homes. I hope you will find that the simple ideas in this book make home life more enjoyable, helping you parents "connect" with your children.

What This Book is For

I believe parents are looking for ideas that provide children with the right kinds of routines, predictability and structure. You may already be doing many things to meet these needs, but I know that a few more good ideas will be of value. You can sometimes fall into great traditions, but many of the best require conscious effort. In this book I will share a broad variety of everyday and holiday activities that have become traditional favorites in our family.

In addition to discussing everyday moments, I have spent a lot of effort assembling fun things to do on holidays. Holidays are also natural occasions for connecting with your children; they give children something to look forward to and depend on in an insecure world. They are often one of the few times families have "time out" together from the cares of the world. Families can come away from holiday celebrations recharged and strengthened because they have been able to focus on what really matters to them in this world—each other. Fond memories of holiday celebrations can last a lifetime, binding family members together and drawing them back to their homes to be together again.

The best family traditions are those which increase love and open communication, strengthen individual family members, build self-esteem and security, and tie generations together. See if some of our traditions spark ideas for your family!

2
Mealtime Traditions

Some say there is no more important time for the family to be together than the daily evening meal. Parents and children can interact in a non-threatening environment in which family members face each other and can talk about their day. Sometimes it takes a bit of creativity and planning to encourage family members to even show up consistently. The right mix of consistency and variety can make this an anticipated event.

Surprise Supper

Once a month, gather for a meal in which each person is responsible to make one course. Then trying to keep their course a secret is part of the fun. Several days before, place meal assignments (for appetizers, main dish, side dishs, salad and dessert) and money for ingredients in envelopes; then have family members draw them from a hat. Besides being a lot of fun, this activity is a good learning experience for children.

The Same Meal Every Week

Having the same meal once each week gives families something consistent to count on. (It also creates one less meal to plan each week!) It doesn't have to be a big production as long as it is something everyone likes, like chicken every Sunday or waffles on Saturday night.

Recipe of the Week

One night each week or month, try a recipe the family has never had before. This gives children something to look forward to, which in this case is variety. Once they get used to the idea that different can be good, children will try harder to be on time for meals, especially if they are not told on which day they will have the surprise recipe. Of course, this may not be true if you tried liverburgers last time! And of course, the experimental dishes shouldn't be presented on a "you have to eat it" basis. This is the family's time to sample, experiment, and acquire new tastes. Let the family vote on whether the menu or recipe should be repeated.

If everybody likes a certain dish, put the recipe in a "favorites" file. You'll have an ever-growing file of dishes the family likes and fewer complaints of "not that again!"

Picnics

If the weather is good, throw a little variety into mealtime by spreading a blanket on the back lawn and letting everyone help take the food outside. It would be an even bigger surprise if on some cold winter night you brought dinner into the living room in a picnic basket. Spread out a blanket and serve foods you usually eat in July. You could even roast hot dogs and marshmallows in your fireplace.

3
Bedtime Traditions
Bedtime For Younger Children

Getting children to sleep can cause more contention than almost anything else. (I speak with the voice of experience.) Bedtime is the time of day when children, especially young children, are most in need of reassurance and comfort. Bedtime will be easier and more meaningful, both for child and parent, if you recognize that you cannot force your child to go to sleep. You can, however, insist that children be in and out of their beds at certain times.

Younger children especially need a bedtime routine to make the transition between day time and sleep time. Allow 30-45 minutes for this process, and it truly is a process. Rushing them off to bed makes them feel insecure and that you are trying to get rid of them—and then they really will not be able to sleep. The following ideas are examples of how to make the most of this time together.

Bedtime Treat

This comforting tradition for little children helps settle them for the night. Each night after your child has put his or her pajamas on, bring in a little tray with a snack and a book for both of you. This tradition helps children actually want to get ready for bed (if you can believe that is possible!). After eating and reading and brushing his or her teeth, your child should be ready to pray and be tucked in.

Storytelling

Many famous children's authors got their start telling stories to their children. You may not capture the world's attention, but you will capture your child's attention if you tell stories at bedtime. My adult children still remember all the details of a series their grandmother made up for them long ago. Younger children love stories that continue night after night.

Children especially love it when you tell stories of your own childhood—it links them with the past. The only thing they love more than that is hearing about their own past. They will ask you over and over about the day they were born and the time they crumbled a whole box of shredded wheat into the rug. Telling these stories confirms your joy from having each child come into your family, and your delight in their individual personalities.

Bedtime for Older Children

Many kids are more willing to talk to parents at bedtime than any other time of day, so never bring up faults or irritations during this important time. Be available to talk to while they are getting ready for bed, letting your children control the direction of conversation.

Waiting up for Teens

You can give your children a sense of security and give yourself peace of mind by waiting up for them to come home, or instructing them to wake you when they arrive. If nothing else, this helps you know your children are safe and at what time they get home. It also helps children feel that someone cares and is looking out for them. It even gives them a weapon to use against peer pressure: "I can't do that because my parents are waiting up for me!" And remember, children may tell you things at 1 a.m. that they would never tell you the next morning!

(This type of rule works best if children understand that you are doing it out of concern for their safety, not because you are suspicious. Children will work hard to maintain or restore trust, but have no incentive to be trustworthy if you are suspicious no matter what they do.)

4
Enjoying The Sabbath

One of the most important tools for keeping families together is not just an idea—it's the Lord's commandment. There is no better day for family members to get closer to God and to each other. Yet, while this quality, unhurried time is difficult to achieve on any other day, it can be equally difficult to find on Sunday unless there is proper planning. Most traditions are easier to start if you establish a set of ground rules the whole family can live with. It can be tricky to maintain the balance between wholesome activities and each child's agency; show by example how spending wholesome time together can help your family call the Sabbath day a "delight."

Sunday Walks with the Children

One of the best things about a walk with one of your children is that the two of you are alone together with no distractions. Little children love to go for a walk to a place special to them, like a park. Teenagers may want to walk with you only after dark! Also, children often talk more freely when they don't have to look you in the face.

A Sunday walk is most effective if you only plan the walk, not the agenda. Let your child talk freely about what he or she wants without correction, criticism, or unwanted advice. You can accomplish much more from simply listening and being available to your child than you ever will by lecturing or prying.

Family Gatherings

Many families gather every Sunday or one Sunday each month to eat pre-prepared meals and to visit together. If you live near relatives, don't pass up the opportunity to be with them on this special day. Doing this gives children a chance to play with their extended family, and they stay close to you rather than going off to friends' houses.

If you live far from relatives, try other traditions that keep the family together during the day. Visit friends together or work on family projects. Schedule a family council or plan service for others.

5
Giving Family Service

Every parent would love for her children to learn the joys of serving others without expecting a reward. However, it can be difficult for children to learn the joys of anonymous service unless someone provides an environment in which they can learn that lesson first-hand. Unfortunately, we often tend to perform acts of charitable service only during the Christmas season or when a need is quite obvious.

Some of the best family bonding moments are not spent together at all but are accomplished individually, in secret. Anonymous service between family members can do wonders for creating a charitable, harmonious home environment. The person attempting to serve others gains a much greater love and sensitivity towards those whom he serves. The recipient of anonymous acts of kindness feels loved and will be more charitable towards others, knowing that any family member could be the doer of good deeds.

The following are variations of ideas normally associated with Christmas. But limiting family service "games" to only one season of the year sends the message that service is only for special occasions. Try one or more of these ideas after a family lesson on service. I would recommend implementing these ideas only periodically—you don't want to send the message that service is something someone organizes for you!

Angel for a Day

Cut small strips of paper, one for each member of your family. Write "Angel" on one of the slips. Place the folded slips in a special container. Each morning, for a week or longer, draw slips. Whomever picks the "Angel" slip is an angel for the day, and performs small acts of kindness and giving in secret.

Special-Friend Calling Cards

Set aside an envelope for each member of the family. Place five or six black gift tags in each envelope except one, in which you place five or six gift tags that say "Your Special Friend was here." Whomever receives the cards that week performs good deeds, then leaves a calling card!

Secret Helpers

Let everyone draw a name of another family member and be her "secret helper" for a day or a week. That way, every person gets involved in service.

6
Serving Outside the Home

Organized family service projects to others should be ongoing. However, do all you can to ensure that your children don't view service projects as something mom and dad think up to "make the kids learn charity." The important thing is to create an environment in which the children look beyond themselves and experience the joy of filling others' needs.

Let the Children Take Charge

Children get more out of service projects if they help develop the ideas and take charge while parents act only as advisors and helpers. Be sure that the children divide the responsibilities according to the talents, abilities and desires of each family member. No one should feel coerced or shamed into serving.

Find Real Needs

As a family, make a list of people in need that you know, then choose those you feel you could best assist. Do your best to determine real needs—a casserole and cookies don't fit most circumstances. Depending on their needs, do yard work or housework for them, baby sit their children, take them a meal, be their friend, visit them, leave gift boxes anonymously (allowing each family member to donate), take them shopping, or invite them to family activities.

7
Linking Generations

Turn the hearts of your children to their forefathers by helping them learn the heritage laid by their forefathers. Our ancestors shouldn't be discussed only on special occasions, but they deserve a place during everyday conversations. Children will feel more connected to previous generations if you hang pictures of their ancestors in your home, talk about them, and visit the places they lived or their grave sites.

Below are a few ideas which link children to their ancestors, or which may leave a vivid record of your family for future generations. The benefits of preserving memories are not limited to your posterity—the work involved can be quite fun and memorable itself!

Family Tree

Let everyone in the family help construct a family tree to display in your home. It can either be a simple project for an evening or a work of art that is constructed over weeks or months.

Heritage Dinner

Serve a foreign dinner from one of your ancestral countries. One year, our family celebrated a Ukrainian Christmas on January 6th to honor my husband's Ukrainian heritage. With a little research at the library, I was able to serve the traditional twelve-dish Christmas-Eve meal, symbolic of the twelve apostles. I set the table with a Ukrainian embroidered cloth set over a handful of hay to remind us of Christ's birth in the manger. Braided bread with a candle was placed in the center. The kids watched for the first evening star, which is when a Ukrainian family sits down to eat the Holy Supper. My husband began the meal with the traditional greeting, "Khrystos Rodyvsia" (Christ is born), to which we replied, "Slavim Yoho" (Let us glorify Him). Not all our children enjoyed the twelve meatless dishes, but they all gained a greater understanding of their Ukrainian ancestry.

Along with your dinner you could play music of the country; or learn a traditional song; tell a story about your ancestors; or discuss their customs, traditions and way of life. You could also learn a few words of their language and use these during your dinner. The important thing is to not turn this into a social studies class—this is supposed to be fun!

8
Family Media Fun

Family Newspaper

This project is much more than a great way to keep in touch with extended family or family members away from home. Getting the whole family to work together also helps build a sense of family spirit, not to mention helping artistic and writing talents blossom. Appoint an editor and assign reporters to cover business, entertainment, sports, gossip, etc. Publish your newspaper once a year, twice, quarterly, or whenever something newsworthy happens. Children feel important when they know that something is being written by or about them and read by others.

Family Diary

Let family members take turns recording what they think is important for week- or month-long periods. The journal must be kept in a spot accessible to the whole family, as it is meant to be read. Although only one person at a time is responsible for recording events, other family members should also be free to add their own perspectives whenever they wish. A family journal can often function as a safe place for children to share feelings with their parents and siblings. Many people, children included, find it easier to say things in writing. Parents can also make notes of their children's endearing qualities and little triumphs. Family members should be encouraged to keep the journal thoughtful and positive, as it will be shared with posterity.

Making Movies

If you have access to a video camera, you already know how easily memories come back when they are recorded in full-motion color. But have you considered using that expensive piece of equipment for something other than footage of family reunions and Christmas day? Teaching children to responsibly use a video recorder gives them a great tool with which to exercise creativity, learn to work together, and have fun with family members.

Spend time together planning and making movies or commercials, versions of favorite television shows, game shows, talk shows or even dramas. Playing back family movies helps you relive some of your best moments together. How I wish our family's play from our three-year-old's party ("Little Black Riding Hood") was on tape!

9
Preserving Memories

Preserving memories and mementos doesn't come naturally to most children—and it doesn't come naturally to many parents either. Yet we have been admonished to keep a journal and preserve records for posterity. Some of the best methods for preserving memories are also fun and easy with a little preparation.

Saving Mementos

It is much easier to save important items if you keep a file folder for each member of the family in the kitchen or family room. As your children bring things home from school or church, it takes only a moment to put the items in their proper folders for safekeeping. Then periodically, on lazy Sunday afternoons or any time a child seems bored, you can pull out a file and update the journal together. You may end up spending more time looking at old mementos and reminiscing about good times than you will putting it together, but that's time well spent, too. And when your children leave home, their childhood memories and mementos from birth to graduation will be neatly and chronologically arranged in albums.

Scrapbooks and Photo Albums

A book or album shows children that they are so important that someone made a book about them. Pictures can bring back fun family memories and other important events, but don't forget to include your child's report cards, ribbons from field days, pictures from art classes, mementos from special outings, birthday and

Christmas cards, Valentines—anything of significance in your child's life.

I have found that binder-type photo albums with sleeves of different sizes are wonderful for scrapbooks. Certificates, cards and mementoes can simply be slipped into the pockets, which come in different sizes to accommodate pictures. Children's artwork can be hole-punched and slipped in without being put in sleeves. Children can write up memories of important events on notebook paper or journal sheets. Take dictation for children who are too little to write.

Books of Wisdom

When a child is about to leave home for college or a mission, make a small album filled with words of wisdom, including favorite sayings of family members. Or, make a small recipe book of all the family favorites for a child leaving home.

For a preschooler, write the story of your family, putting captions under pictures to make it a picture story. Your creativity and imagination are the only limits! Any of these books could become family heirlooms.

The Birth of a Child

The birth of each child may be memorable to its parents and older siblings, but I guarantee that the newborn isn't going to keep any records of it. Only you can preserve a record of this important event for your child as he grows up.

Birth Tree

Plant a tree for each child when he or she is born. Not only does this give children a tangible, growing symbol to relate to, but it shows that they were wanted, that their birth was an important event. When old enough, allow each child to care for his or her tree.

A Letter to Your Baby

Write a letter to your new baby as soon as possible after his or her birth. Express your feelings about having him or her join your family, including the story of his entry into the world. Describe the day he was born, the trip to the hospital, your first thoughts when you saw him, etc. Read this letter to your child when he or she is old enough to appreciate it.

Time Capsule

Pack a time capsule shortly after the birth of each child and present it at graduation. Include a copy of the day's newspaper, a TV guide, a grocery flier, a sale flier showing the day's clothing fashions, and anything else that might be interesting in 18 years.

Birthdays

Celebrating children's birthdays reinforces their feelings of importance to the family. Besides the traditional birthday party, many other fun things can make the birthday boy or girl feel special.

Birthday Morning

Make it a tradition to decorate a birthday child's room while he is asleep or at school. Enlist the help of anyone who wants to decorate. One year my son's friends strung crepe paper streamers all over his room to form a giant basket which they filled with dozens of balloons. He couldn't even get into his room. He loved it.

Birthday Tablecloth

Purchase or make a light-colored tablecloth before your child's first birthday. At each birthday dinner, allow each guest to write his name or a message on it using a special fabric pen (make sure you have first placed newspapers under the cloth to protect the table).

Start in the center of the tablecloth and work out as the years go by. This will give your child a unique record of his birthdays.

Birthday Trees

One year I made a birthday tree for one of my children. It was such a hit that I had to make one for each of our other children as their birthdays came along. My little kids had as much fun helping make them as they did getting their own.

A birthday tree is simply a large tree branch that you anchor in a pot and decorate. Hang treats of all kinds, tiny presents and homemade cards. Decorate according to a theme that your child is interested in. Your tree will look pretty if you add bows, tiny balloons or other decorations.

Birthday Compliments

Instead of simply letting the birthday child unwrap his or her gifts, have a tradition that the giver of the gift gives a compliment along with the package. Hopefully, this will help your children learn that saying nice things to each other is not fatal.

Birthday Picture

Take a full-body picture of each child on his or her birthday, each standing in the same spot if possible. Not only do children love to see how much they have grown, but this practice provides an interesting record for posterity—especially if your child continues this through adulthood.

King/Queen for a Day

Make a birthday crown for the birthday person to wear on his or her day. A sturdy one can be used for years; in fact, it may become a family heirloom. The King or Queen has certain "royal birthday privileges" such as ordering breakfast in bed, assigning his chores to one of his subjects, and so on.

Celebrity Birthday Party

Celebrate the birthday of one of your children's favorite heroes to surprise them (make sure the hero is one you want to encourage). My daughter is *crazy* about the books of Lucy Maud Montgomery, so on a November 30th I surprised her with a dinner to celebrate the Author's birthday. I made an Anne of Green Gables cake using a book-shaped cake pan and made foods mentioned in the author's books. Place cards were folded paper "books" bearing titles of Lucy's books. For an afternoon of work I was well rewarded by my daughter's delight. I believe it made my daughter feel valued and important, and I know it strengthened our relationship.

Letters from the Tooth Fairy

Losing a tooth is a major milestone in a child's life, so celebrate it with a visit from the Tooth Fairy (she always leaves a letter and money at our house). My children have looked forward to the letters as much as they have anticipated the money. Writing these letters also gives the "Tooth Fairy" a chance to use the left side of her brain and say some nice things about her children anonymously.

First Day of School Cone

The first day of school is a major milestone in a child's life, a day that deserves to be recognized. A delightful German tradition makes children feel special during this time which can be both exciting and stressful for them. Many German parents present their children with a very large paper cone filled with candies, cookies, and treats the morning of the first day of school each year. (If the idea of starting off your child's first week of school with a sugar-high doesn't appeal to you, fill the cone with books, school-supply extras and little toys.)

Directions:

1. To make the cone, which is traditionally about two feet high, cut a very large piece of poster paper into a four-foot diameter circle.
2. Cut a pie-shaped wedge out and roll the circle into your desired cone shape (don't make it too wide at the top!). Tape, glue or staple the sides together to secure it. Make a handle out of two or more layers of the remaining poster paper or out of cardboard. Staple it to the cone near the top of the opening.
3. Decorate the outside of the cone as desired.
4. Line the inside with floral tissue, fastening it to the cone with glue. Leave enough extra tissue at the top to tie it shut. Fill it with desired goodies and tie with a ribbon.

10
New Year's Activities

New Year's is a time to reminisce over the year's highlights—the growth and achievements of family members, news of the extended family, and events around the world. It is a time for soul searching and making resolutions for the year ahead. It is also a time when all soothsayers print out their annual list of predictions. What a golden opportunity for strengthening family relationships through reminiscing together, setting family and individual goals for the year ahead and having fun together around the Wassail bowl!

Giving End-of-Year Recognition

A child's sense of self-worth can be greatly enhanced by occasional outward recognition for achievements or good deeds. While you should avoid giving children an unhealthy appetite or a dependence on praise, it's more likely that you provide too little praise most of the time. Children need both public and private acknowledgement that they are good people and that you and their siblings are proud of them.

Letters to Children

At the end of the year (or any time you like), write a special letter to each child. Share reminiscences of the past year and some of your favorite memories with them. Share your joy in knowing them, and tell them why you are proud of who they are. Your children will read their letters over and over as they get older, so be sure to help them put the letters away for safekeeping.

Award Ceremony

The end of the year is a good time for handing out awards to recognize the progress family members have made or to recognize their endearing traits. Individual awards can either be thought up by the parents, or the whole family can "nominate" family members for awards during the week after Christmas. Awards can take the form of paper scrolls, certificates, homemade plaques, tiny mementos, or large cookies with the award written in icing.

Predictions

Gather around a big bowl of punch and have everyone make a fun prediction for the coming year. Children love the self-acknowledgment that comes from hearing family members discuss their lives.

Predictions can be serious or humorous, but do not allow any that are cutting or tasteless. Go around several times if interest is high. After the predictions are recorded, ceremoniously seal them away in a special envelope to be opened at a party the next year.

Reminiscences

Spend an unhurried, unstructured evening at home around the fireplace munching on snacks as you share favorite memories of the past year. Although this could be very informal (no instructions or introduction), setting the atmosphere and starting with some of your own memories should spark memories for the rest of the family. This type of activity has the potential to be quite memorable itself.

Decorating Tips

The New Year's Tree

Extend the usefulness of your Christmas tree by redecorating it for New Year's Eve. It doesn't take long and it will help shake off those post-Christmas blues. The children will love it. Leave on the lights and tinsel, but exchange the Christmas balls and decorations with any or all of the following:

* *Balloons:* Place very small balloons among the branches.
* *Noisemakers:* Tie party noisemakers on with green and white ribbons.
* *Good Luck-Coins:* Using a glue gun or scotch tape, attach a gold cord to foil-covered chocolate coins and hang them on the tree.
* *Wish Cards:* (These are a neat way to extend your good wishes for the coming year to your family. Directions follow below.)

1. Cut a 2" square card for each member of your family and write a wish on each one. These should be sincere wishes that express one of their greatest needs.
2. Prepare a tiny envelope for each wish card by using the envelope pattern. Trace the pattern, cut it out, and fold it along the fold lines. Glue it together, leaving the top flap free. Use a small hole punch to make a hole in the top left-hand corner.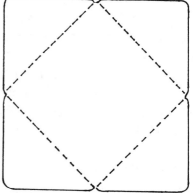
3. Insert wish cards into the envelopes. Write the recipient's name on the front and decorate them. Run a gold cord or ribbon through the hole and attach each envelope to your New Year's tree, or place the cards on pillows after everyone is asleep.

Countdown to Midnight

Why not invite close friends or relatives to bring the whole family and join you for New Year's Eve! If your children are too young to stay up until midnight, just turn the clock ahead a bit. As the midnight hour approaches, the festivities begin. Be prepared with the items listed below. Be sure to have the countdown to midnight in unison at 10 seconds to the hour. Then toss the streamers, blow the horns, break the balloons and sing Auld Lang Syne.

- *Streamers:* Cut streamers out of crepe paper and roll them up.
- *Noisemakers:* Purchase them or use ordinary items around the house. If available, consult a two-year-old—they are experts at creating noisemakers out of ordinary objects.
- *Money Balloons:* Before blowing up balloons, put money in some of them. The more balloons with money, the more fun! Rub the balloons against a sweater or other object to charge them with static electricity, then cover a whole wall with them. At the stroke of midnight announce that there is money in some of the balloons. This will ensure that the new year comes in with a bang!

Letting in the New Year

Here's an old tradition to pass down to your children. In our family my mother would always fling open the front door at the stroke of midnight to let in the new year. According to tradition she should have also opened the back door to let the old year out and said, "Letting out the old, letting in the new."

Family Games

Resolutions

Pass out papers and pencils. Instruct everyone to write out three of their New Year's resolutions. Collect all the papers in a hat and mix them up. Pass the hat around and have each person pick a resolution, read it aloud and guess who made it. Continue until the hat is empty. Keep score to see who correctly guesses the most.
Variation: When people guess correctly, let them keep reading resolutions until they miss one.

If the handwriting on the resolutions gives away the family member, let one person read all of them, then let family members guess who made them.

The Year in Review

Make up a list of questions recalling important family milestones, parents' and childrens' idiosyncrasies and humorous events from the past year. Be sure to give each child equal attention. Answers can be given orally or written if the children are older. Give a prize to the family member with the best memory.

Food Fun

Fortune-Telling Cake

1. Bake your favorite layer or 9" x 13" cake and let it cool.
2. Wash and dry the following fortune-telling items, then poke at least one of each into the cake:
* *Ring*—faithfulness
* *Coin*—riches
* *Dried bean*—wisdom
* *Thimble*—patience
* *Paper Heart*—love
3. Frost the cake, then cut it into equal portions. Tell family members that there are items in the cake, then let each point to the piece they want. Do not let anyone eat the cake until all the fortune-telling items are found. Be extra careful with small children.

Leaf Cookies

These cookies symbolize turning over a new leaf and have funny resolutions written on them.

Directions:

1. Mix your favorite rolled-sugar-cookie dough. Roll it out over pieces of aluminum foil.
2. Trace a leaf pattern onto waxed paper or ordinary writing paper and cut it out.

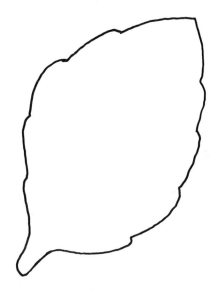

3. Lay the pattern on top of the dough and cut the leaves out with a sharp paring knife. Lift the excess dough away.
4. Place the piece of foil directly onto the cookie sheet. Bake.
5. Lift the foil off the cookie sheet and cool the cookies on wire racks. When cool, remove the cookies from the foil and pipe funny resolutions on with green icing.

Clock Cakes

Batter for a two-layer cake makes two clock cakes.

1. Bake your favorite one-layer cake, or bake it in two 9"-round layer cake pans. Let it cool on wire racks.
2. Cover two cardboard circles (traced from the *bottom* of the cake tins) with aluminum foil. Place the cooled cakes on them.
3. Frost each layer with butter frosting. Immediately place a saucepan lid (approximately 7" in diameter) on top of the cake. Center it so you can decorate the border and sides of the cake with colored sprinkles before the icing sets. Coat the cake evenly, then remove the lid.
4. Pipe on the clock face. You may want to use candies or candles for the numbers and licorice for the hands.

11
Epiphany (Twelfth Day) Traditions

January 6th is called *Twelfth Day, Three King's Day* and *Epiphany* (pronounced ih-PIHF-uh-nee). Epiphany is a holy festival observed by many countries to honor the visit of the Wise Men (the Magi) to the baby Jesus.

Epiphany is a Greek word meaning "manifestation" or "showing." The Feast of the Epiphany acknowledges Christ's first appearance to the Gentile world.

This celebration is an opportunity to teach children the true story of the Wise Men's visit and to correct their misconceptions. The scriptures are silent regarding the names of the wise men, how many there were, and their status in life. Nor were they at the manger the night Jesus was born, as is often depicted in Christmas cards. Although they arrived possibly months later after a long journey, the important thing is to emphasize that then and now, wise men seek Jesus.

Technically, Twelfth Night is January 5th, and January 6th is called Twelfth Day, marking the end of the Christmas Season.

Family Activities

The Wise Men's Journey

When setting up your nativity scene, rather than placing the wise men around the stable, set them a distance away. Family members may take turns moving them a little closer to the stable each day until Epiphany, when they finally reach the Christ Child.

Epiphany Cake

People in many countries eat a Cake of the Kings, or a Twelfth Night Cake in honor of the Three Wise Men. The story of their visit is told. Some people decorate the cake with a crown, while others place three candles on it to represent three magi. Drop a large dried bean into the cake batter before baking. Whoever finds the bean is crowned the Epiphany king or queen, and rules over the evening's festivities. A large paper crown is placed on his/her head, and that person decides what games will be played and who will clean up.

12
Chinese New Year

Celebrating the holidays of other countries teaches children to appreciate other cultures. The Chinese have many delightful traditions that can be used to teach valuable lessons.

For about 4,000 years the Chinese used the ancient lunar calendar which was based on the waxing and waning of the moon. In 1912 they adopted the Gregorian calendar, yet they continue to celebrate the traditional lunar year. The Chinese New Year falls on the day when the second new moon rises after December 22, sometime between January 21 and February 19. Celebrations continue until the next full moon rises.

Decorating

Let the whole family have fun decorating for the holiday, or let one of your children help you make a surprise party for the rest of the family.

Chinese New Year's Scroll

Red is the predominate decorating color because it signifies luck and happiness. Anciently, it was believed that evil spirits fear the color red, so it was used to drive them away. Red streamers, scrolls and banners are hung in the streets and inside homes, es-

especially over doorways, where good luck is said to enter. Make a scroll by writing "GUN HAY FAT CHOY" (Happy New Year) in gold ink on a strip of red poster paper. Decorate with Chinese characters if you wish. Wrap the ends of the paper around dowels or cardboard tubes and tape them together. Hang them with a gold or red cord.

Money Tree

During this holiday tradition, a branch from a cypress or pine tree is brought inside and decorated with coins and other ornaments. Money trees are considered a symbol of prosperity for the new year.

Chinese Lanterns

On the night of the full moon, "The Festival of the Lanterns" is held, during which lanterns of every shape are carried through the streets on bamboo poles. You can purchase Chinese lanterns, but you may decide that it's more fun to have a lantern-making session with the family. When finished, string a line of miniature Christmas lights across the dining room and suspend a row of lanterns from them for your special Chinese New Year Dinner.

Materials Needed:
- one 8 1/2" x 11" sheet of red-and-yellow-print gift wrap, wallpaper or construction paper (one per lamp)
- scissors
- hot glue gun
- stapler
- hanging cord to match paper (optional)
- yellow or gold fringe, braid (optional)

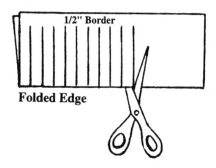

Directions:

1. Fold in half an 8 1/2" x 11" or larger sheet of paper. Cut 18 slits, starting at folded edge and ending 1/2" before the end of the sheet.

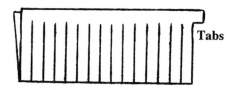

2. Snip off the last cut to make the tabs.

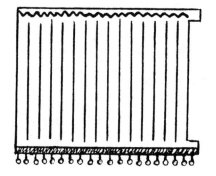

3. Unfold the paper. Open the lantern out flat. Glue the fringe onto the bottom. Glue the braid on the top, or decorate as desired.

4. Glue the tabs in place to form a circle, according to figure. Press down the paper at the folds until the lamp is desired shape. Attach a handle made from cord or matching paper.

Gift Ideas

Ya Sway Chien

On the first day of the Chinese New Year, children find little red envelopes or packets containing money under their pillows. They spend this money during the New Year holiday. Wrap some coins in red paper and surprise your children.

Presents

Chinese families exchange gifts on the last day of the year. Tradition requires that the recipient return a portion of the gift to show his unworthiness to receive it. Teach your children this tradition on the night before they find the packets of money under their pillows. After your children unwrap their red packets of money, again remind them of this Chinese tradition.

Family Activities

Spring Cleaning

It is an ancient custom to thoroughly clean, paint, and repair your house for the new year, thus sweeping away past misfortune. What a novel way to get kids working!

Greeting

Start the day off by greeting your family in your best Chinese accent with "Gun hay fat choy," which means, "I wish you a prosperous New Year. Wish them success in all their undertakings, and with them a long line of descendants—ten thousand generations!

Confucius Says

Tell your family about the most influential philosopher in Chinese history—Confucius. He believed society should emphasize sincerity in private and public conduct, and that the key to an orderly society was in being gentlemanly. He defined a gentleman not as a person of noble birth, but a person of good moral character. Confucius gave many rules of good conduct in the form of sayings. Nowadays, his rules are prefaced with, "Confucius says . . . " If you feel a need for more gentlemanly conduct in your home, see if Confucius can help you. Ask each member of the family what they think needs the most work in the family. Ask each person to write a "Confucius says . . ." rule that, if followed, would solve this problem. After everyone reads theirs, have a vote to determine which one you want to work on first. Post the "Confucius says" rule on the fridge. Whenever anyone slips up, family members are to quote the saying to them. Sometimes humor will work where other methods will not.

All-Night Party

This might be the one night of the year in which you allow your children to stay up as late as they want. A Chinese superstition states that the longer the children stay awake on New Year's Eve, the longer the parents will live! Strike a deal and let them keep this tradition as a reward for honoring the spring cleaning custom!

Food Fun

Chinese Dinner

Serve your family a Chinese dinner and eat with chopsticks! Cover the table with a red cloth and candles, and serve twelve vegetarian courses if you wish. Play games and ask riddles between courses.

Chinese Fortune Cookies

It's fun to make your own fortune cookies because you can personalize the fortunes and make them humorous.

Directions:

1. Cut strips of paper about 3" wide by 2" long. Write fortunes on the paper strips. Fold in half and set them aside.
2. Beat three egg whites until frothy.
3. Add and beat until dissolved:
     2/3 cup white sugar
     1/8 tsp. salt
     1/4 tsp. vanilla
4. Mix in until well blended:
     1/2 cup melted butter or margarine
5. Stir in 1 cup white flour until smooth
6. Chill the mixture, covered, for at least 30 minutes.
7. Place rounded teaspoons of the batter on to a greased cookie sheet. Using the back of the spoon, spread out the batter to form 3" circles.
8. Bake only two or three cookies at a time. Bake them at 350 degrees for 3-5 minutes or until edges are golden brown.
9. Working quickly, remove one cookie at a time from the sheet. While holding it in the palm of your hand, place a fortune strip in the center. Fold the cookie in half, then fold it again to place it in a muffin tin. The muffin cup will keep the cookie folded until it sets. The cookies must be shaped while they are hot. If the

cookies become too brittle to fold, they can be returned to the oven for a minute to soften them.

10. Continue until all the batter is used up.

13
Valentine's Day

No other holiday better lends itself to beautiful and sentimental expressions of love than Valentine's Day. Here's a chance to craft, create and share love as a family.

Gift Ideas

Love Letters

We often wrongly assume that our loved-ones know how much they mean to us. However, there are times when each of us need encouragement or reassurance that we are loved. Letter writing is a special way to express love because a letter is a treasure that can be read over and over.

Especially-For-You Funny Valentines

It's fun to make a silly Valentine for each member of your family with a rhyme that pokes fun at them. Make it a tradition. Decorate the Valentines with stickers.

Roses are red
Violets are blue
You'll still be my baby
When you're 92!

Roses are red,
Violets are blue,
I'm stuck on you, dear
Like a blonde
Blob of glue!

Victorian Love Boxes

These little boxes are made solely for the purpose of holding tiny love notes. Children can easily create. They may spend a lot of time creating a work of art.

1. Gather up some small boxes of different shapes and sizes.
2. Cut cupids, hearts, and flowers from old greeting cards, Valentines and gift wrap.
3. Gather up doilies, old pieces of jewelry that are fairly flat, pretty buttons, bits of lace, rickrack and ribbon, decals and hearts of all kinds.

When you have a nice collection, start cutting and gluing, covering the whole outside of your box with a collage.

To fill the little boxes as a family, have each family member write something he/she enjoys about each member of the family on a slip of colored paper. Put each person's notes in her respective box. For a special gift, fill each with dozens of notes. Each member of the family gets a love box filled with little love notes to read on cloudy days.

Heart Pockets

Heart pockets can show up anywhere—on children's pillows, on the breakfast table or in coat pockets or lunch bags. They are easy and fun to make.

Directions:

1. Cut two hearts of the same size from construction paper, gift wrap, or anything you choose.
2. Decorate one of the hearts.
3. Spread glue along the edges of the bottom heart, as shown by the dotted line.
4. Glue the top heart in place to form a pocket. Let the glue dry.
5. Slip a little gift, candy or love note inside!

Valentine Mail Box

This nostalgic centerpiece can hold a Valentine or gift for each member of your family. You may have learned to make these in grade school. Simply choose an appropriate-sized box, tape the top shut and cut a slot in the top big enough for your gifts to go through. Cover the box with Valentine gift wrap or with any plain paper you can decorate.

Directions:

1. Next, to prepare your gifts or Valentines, punch a hole in each one and attach a 24" to 36" ribbon.

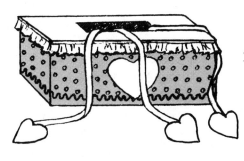

2. On the free end of each ribbon, attach small hearts with family member's names written on them.

3. Drop the Valentines or gifts into the mailbox and leave the tiny hearts dangling out on the table. If the ribbons are long enough they can reach out to each person's place at the table.

4. On Valentine's Day, everyone pulls their ribbon to receive their Valentine or gift.

Danish Woven Hearts Filled With Love

Materials:

- lightweight cardboard to trace the pattern on
- red and white lightweight poster paper, or glazed paper such as origami
- scissors
- pencil

Directions:

1. Trace the pattern onto cardboard and cut it out.
2. Fold red and white papers in half. Place the pattern on the paper, putting the bottom edge on the fold. Trace and cut it out. Accuracy is very important.
3. Place the folded halves side by side (as illustrated). Weave the strips around and through each other—not just over and under.

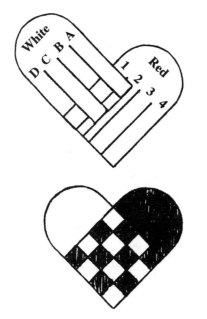

To Begin:

Poke row 1 between the top and bottom layers of row A.

Open row 1 and slip row B through. Poke row 1 between the top and the bottom layers of row cup.

Open row 1 and slip row D through. Pull up to make it fit snugly.

Begin the next row by slipping Row A between the top and bottom layers of row two. Continue weaving until your heart looks like the illustration.

4. Open the heart. Line it with a lace paper doily, colored cellophane or tissue paper. A handle can be attached or bows glued on.

5. Fill your heart basket with homemade treats, candy, or small gifts. Tuck in love notes with the treats.

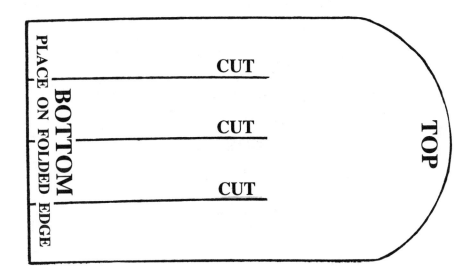

Family Activities

Valentine-Making Night

Creating provides an escape from the rest of the world, eases tensions and gives a feeling of satisfaction. Creating together, you may find yourselves swapping stories, jokes and having an old-fashioned good time. Here are a few ideas to get you started.

Candy-Gram Valentines

Send a Valentine greeting of wrapped candies and chocolate bars that make up parts of the message. Use stiff cardboard for the valentine. A glue gun secures the treat wrapper directly onto the card.

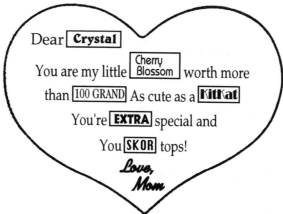

Spatter Valentines

1. Fold a piece of art paper in half to form a card shape, or start with a purchased blank.
2. Cut out a heart shape from a piece of paper and lay it on the blank card. Place the card on a large piece newspaper to protect the floor from paint.

3. Spatter paint the card by dipping an old toothbrush into watered-down poster or acrylic paint and rubbing a knife over the bristles. Wear an old shirt to protect your clothing. You may want to spatter the card with several different colors.
4. Let dry before removing the loose heart.

5. Add additional decorations such as stickers, buttons, tiny bows or Valentine pictures cut from old cards.

6. Don't discard the cut-out heart. Use it to decorate a blank card.

True Love Knot Valentine

Before there were traditional Valentines, love knots were given as tokens of love. Love messages were written on loops of the ribbon. They were called Endless-Love Knots because they had no beginning or end, symbolizing eternal love. Love knots became a main design on early Valentines.

To make a love knot, trace the pattern on white paper, cut it out and attach it to a colored heart or card. Complete by writing your love message on the loops.

Edible Valentines (Big Cookie Hearts)

1. Mix up your favorite rolled cookie dough.
2. Lay out a cookie sheet-sized piece of aluminum foil, sprinkle the foil lightly with flour. For each cookie, roll out about a cup of chilled dough onto the foil.
3. Cut out a paper heart the size you want your cookie to be. Place it on the dough. Cut around it with a sharp knife. Lift off the pattern and remove the excess dough.
4. If you want to tie a ribbon or two on your heart, make holes with a plastic drinking straw.
5. Place the aluminum foil on a cookie sheet and bake until done. Watch carefully.
6. Lift aluminum foil off cookie sheet and set it on wire racks to cool. Reopen straw holes while cookie is still warm. Do not remove the foil until the cookie is completely cooled.
7. Cut out small hearts of different sizes from leftover dough to use as decoration for your big hearts.
8. Decorate with icing, small cookie hearts, candies and ribbons.

Valentine's Day Dinner

Do something special in the kitchen, whether it be a special dessert or one of these dinners.

Black Tie Dinner

What better day is there to plan a truly elegant dinner? You can either plan a romantic dinner for two or a formal dinner for the whole family. Either way, go all-out—formal dress, candlelight, flowers, soft music, fine china, before dinner drink, polite discussion and manners! Talk a friend or a relative into being your waiter. Plan an elegant menu you can prepare mostly in advance. In this atmosphere your children will be very receptive to learning proper table etiquette.

Fireplace Picnic

Eating by firelight is very romantic. Pack a big picnic basket, including something elegant (no banana boats here). The following punch container idea can help set the mood.

Flower and Foliage Ice Bottle

(This is very easy and elegant).

Materials:
- half gallon cardboard milk container
- leaves, ferns, flower petals
- an empty bottle taller than the milk carton, but which fits inside

1. Open the top of the milk carton
2. Place the empty bottle inside
3. Put several inches of water in the milk carton
4. Arrange your foliage and flowers; placing stems in the water until all sides are covered.
5. Fill with water, leaving the neck of bottle exposed. Set something heavy on top to keep the bottle immersed. Freeze.
6. When ready to use, tear away the milk carton. Fill the bottle with punch or juice. Place in a dish or basket lined with a cloth or a napkin.

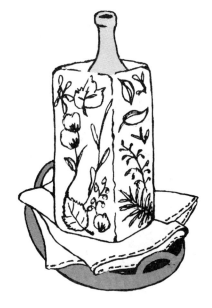

Food Fun

Sweetheart Luncheon

Make heart-shaped place mats and matching napkins from Valentine fabric. Tie the napkins with bows in place of napkin rings. Use tiny gifts wrapped in Valentine designs as the place cards. A Valentine Mail Box holding a Valentine for each participant could serve as the table centerpiece. Preparing for the luncheon will be half the fun. Serve theme foods such as heart-shaped sandwiches, fluffy fruit salads, pink mints and cream puffs.

Heart Sandwiches

Freeze loaves of white and whole wheat bread. Cut the bread while frozen using round and heart-shaped cutters (you need two sizes of heart-shaped cookie cutters). Mix white and dark breads as shown, replacing cutout hearts in the dark bread with white hearts and vice versa.

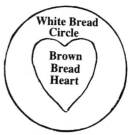

Hearts and Bows Cookies

1. Prepare your favorite cutout cookie recipe. Cut out heart shapes.
2. Make two holes in each heart with the blunt end of a wooden skewer or a drinking straw, as shown in diagram. Bake. Reopen the holes while cookies are still warm.

3. After the cookies cool, run ribbons through the holes and tie bows. Decorate with icing.

Heart Croustades

(Serve any creamed food, scrambled eggs or stew in these attractive bread cases.)

1. Preheat the oven to 375 degrees
2. Choose a loaf of unsliced day-old bread. Slice the bread 1 1/2" thick.
3. Place the heart pattern on bread slice and cut it out with a sharp knife.
4. Hollow out the center, leaving a 1/4" thick "wall" all around.
5. Brush it with melted butter and bake it on a cookie sheet 12-15 minutes, or until golden brown.
6. Fill it with food immediately and serve hot.

Frothy Pink Punch

(Pretty and pink for your Valentine table!)

1. Combine in a punch bowl:
     1 pt. vanilla ice cream
     1 pt. raspberry sherbet
2. Stir to make it smooth, then add:
     4 cups raspberry cocktail or juice
     4 cups ginger ale (or to taste)

Heart-Shaped cupcakes (makes 14 or 15)

You don't need a special tin to make these heart-shaped cupcakes—just aluminum foil. They are so easy that even small cooks will be pleased with their results.

1. Heat oven to 350 degrees.
2. Measure into mixing bowl:
    1 cup cake flour (or place 2 Tablespoons of cornstarch in bottom of a cup and fill it with all-purpose flour)
    1/2 tsp. baking powder
    1/2 tsp. salt
    1/2 tsp. soda
    1/4 cup cocoa
    3/4 cup white sugar
3. Stir the above ingredients thoroughly, then add:
    1/4 cup shortening
    1/4 cup water
    1/2 tsp. vanilla
    6 T. sour milk
4. Beat the above ingredients for two minutes, scraping the bowl often. Add:

Foil Balls

1 egg, unbeaten
1 egg yolk
Beat all ingredients one minute
5. Fill the lined muffin tins half full. Place small balls of crumpled foil between each liner and the pan cups to achieve the "heart" shape.
6. Bake approx. 25 minutes. Place on wire rack to cool.
7. Decorate the cupcakes by frosting their tops with pink icing. Then tint the icing darker pink or use white frosting and pipe it around the edge of the cupcakes to define the heart shapes. Top them with sprinkles or Valentine candy.

Black Forest Valentine Cake

1. Bake your favorite chocolate cake in one 9"x 9" square pan and one 9" round pan. Let them cool completely on wire racks.
2. Trace a heart-shaped base from a large cardboard box to assemble the cake on. Use an empty 9" square cake pan to trace the bottom of the heart. Use an empty 9" round pan to trace the top sides, as shown in the illustration. Cut out the base and cover it with aluminum foil. Place lace paper doilies on top so that the edges show when the cake is set on top.
3. Cut the round cake in half and assemble as shown.
4. To decorate the cake you will need:

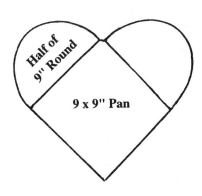

   1/2 T. maraschino cherry juice
   1/4 cup chocolate syrup
   19 oz. can cherry pie filling
   2 cups whipping cream (whipped and sweetened)
   Chocolate for curls
   mini chocolate hearts or other candies for decorating.

Sprinkle the cake with cherry juice then spread on the chocolate sauce. Use about half the whipped cream to frost the entire cake smoothly. Stir the cherry pie filling until smooth and spread it into a heart shape on the top of the cake, leaving a 2" border all around.

Put the remaining whipped cream into a pastry bag and pipe a border around the top and bottom edge of the cake. Pipe a large heart in the middle of the cherry pie filling and fill it in.

Garnish the cake with cherries, chocolate curls, miniature chocolate hearts or candies. Refrigerate until served.

14
Saint Patrick's Day

St. Patrick's Day is celebrated on March 17 to honor someone who most historians agree was not Irish, was not named Patrick, did not drive snakes from Ireland, didn't bring Christianity to the island, and wasn't even born on March 17! But don't let any of that spoil your family's fun. This is a day when everyone can call himself Irish, wear green, and have some clean fun. Make the most of this day with your family!

Limericks

A limerick is a five-line humorous verse with an a-a-b-b-a rhyming pattern. The name is derived from the city of Limerick in Ireland. They are especially entertaining when you write them about members of your family and poke a little fun at them. Surprise family members on St. Patrick's Day by writing each one a playful limerick on a green paper shamrock.

There was a young
Man named Mark,
Who was constantly
off on a lark.
Whether jogging and biking
Snowboarding and hiking
No one saw him from morning to dark!

Blarney Stone Centerpiece

This is a great conversation starter. Here is a wee bit of history you can share with the family when they ask why you have a rock on the dinner table. The real blarney stone is a block of limestone set into a tower of the Blarney Castle near Cork, Ireland. Legend has it that anyone who kisses the stone receives the gift of expressive, flattering speech.

Any flat gray rock can be used for your blarney stone. Dress it up a wee bit by surrounding it with a border of shamrocks and white ribbon, or lay it on a nest of crumpled green tissue. Underneath the rock place a blarney message for each member of the family. These should be the most extravagant compliments you can think of, but they must be sincere. Emphasize actions, not character. A variation on this idea is to have everyone kiss the blarney stone before dinner and then speak in expressive, flattering speech for the whole dinner. See "Blarney Stone Centerpiece."

Family Activities

Limerick Writing

Have all family members put their names in a hat. Each participant draws a name and writes a limerick about that person. Read them aloud.

Wearing of the Green

Almost all families follow this tradition. If you don't wear something green you receive a pinch!

Family Games

Have a little St. Patrick's Day party for your young children and play these games.

Who Goes there?

One person is chosen to be the leprechaun. He/she sits blindfolded on a chair with a bag of gold (use chocolate coins) at his feet.

Everyone else sits on the floor several yards behind the leprechaun in a semi-circle.

One parent taps a child on the back and he becomes the thief. The thief's objective is to be so quiet that he can steal the leprechaun's gold and get back to his seat without being heard. However, if the leprechaun hears the thief and asks "Who goes there?", the thief must stop in his tracks and answer in a disguised voice: "Leprechaun, Leprechaun, I've Come to Steal Your Gold!"

If the leprechaun can guess who the thief is, the thief becomes the new leprechaun. If not, another thief is appointed and the game continues.

Pot-of-Gold Game

Leprechauns are noted for being bad-tempered and full of tricks. According to legend, if you catch one and never take your eyes off him, he must lead you to his pot of gold. You must be mighty clever because you can never trust a leprechaun. They seem to get away just when you think you're going to be rich.

To play this game, you need a pot of gold. (Chocolate coins add more fun to the game because there really is a reward at the end.) To start, one person is chosen to be the leprechaun. Everyone else is taken to another room while the leprechaun hides the pot of gold. When the others return the game is played just like "Hot and Cold." The first person to find the pot of gold is the next leprechaun. When you get tired of playing, divide up the gold.

Food Fun

A favorite St. Patrick's Day tradition in many families is to serve all green foods and shape everything you possibly can like a Shamrock. Below is a bit of both.

Shamrock Pancakes for Breakfast

Add green food coloring to the batter. Pour the batter onto the griddle in a shamrock shape: pour three small circles close together and add a short stem.

Lime Sodas

Place two or three scoops of vanilla ice cream in a tall glass, then fill the glass with lime soda. Insert a straw and a long-handled spoon.

Choco-Mint Pie

1. Make the crust for a 9" pie by mixing:
   3 T. melted butter
   1 1/4 cup crushed chocolate wafer cookies (reserve 2 T. of mixture for garnish)
2. Melt in double boiler:
   2 cups white miniature marshmallows (or 24 large white marshmallows)
   3/4 cup milk
3. Let cool, then fold in thoroughly:
   3/4 tsp. peppermint extract (or to taste)
   green food coloring
   1 cup whipping cream, whipped
4. Pour into the pie shell. Sprinkle reserved crumbs on top. Freeze until firm. Keep cold until serving.

Shamrock Rolls

1. Make yeast mixture by dissolving:
   1/2 cup lukewarm water (110 degrees)
   3/4 tsp. sugar
   1 T. yeast
2. Meanwhile, mix in large bowl:
   1/2 cup scalded milk
   heaping 1/4 cup margarine
   1/2 cup water
   1/4 cup sugar
   1/4 tsp. salt
   1 egg, beaten
3. Beat in:
   Risen yeast mixture
   1 cup flour
4. Add flour and knead until the dough is soft, not stiff. Knead well. Place the dough in a buttered bowl. Turn the dough in the bowl to butter the top. Let it rise, covered with a clean towel, until it's double in size.
5. Shape the dough into 1" balls. Place 3 balls in each greased muffin cup. Let them rise until they have doubled in volume.
6. Bake them at 375 degrees for 10 to 12 min.
   Makes 2 dozen.

15
Easter

Easter is a special holiday with great spiritual significance. It is hoped that the fun holiday traditions offered here will in no way overshadow spiritual traditions that help your family grow in love and appreciation for the Savior.

Easter-Egg Tree

An Easter tree displays your beautifully decorated Easter eggs. Anchor a pretty branch in a pot of gravel, rocks or plaster of Paris. Let everyone hang blown eggs on the branches. (Cooked ones are too heavy; directions for blown eggs follow.) Add miniature baskets filled with tiny eggs, chicks on nests, small rabbits, etc.

Easter Basket

Decorate a big glorious basket to hold all the colored eggs the family makes. Let them see their work on display.

All About Eggs

The best way to hard-boil eggs: place the eggs in a saucepan and cover them completely with cold water. Slowly bring the water to a boiling point. Cover the pan and lower the heat to keep the water just below its simmering point. Set your timer for 25 minutes. Drain and chill the eggs in cold water immediately when the timer rings.

Caution: Cooked eggs spoil rapidly at room temperature. If you intend to eat the eggs you decorate, keep them refrigerated. Do not eat eggs that have been decorated with felt-tipped pens, as the dye often goes through the eggshell and is harmful unless the pen is labeled non-toxic.

How to blow an egg: using a large needle, poke a hole in each end of a raw egg. Enlarge one of the holes a bit by breaking off tiny bits of the shell with the needle point. Insert a needle and wiggle it around to break up the yolk. Shake the egg. Place a drinking straw against the smaller hole and blow through it to expel the egg out the larger hole. Rinse the shell thoroughly and store it in an egg carton. Blown eggs may be too delicate for young children to decorate.

How to hang a blown egg: break a wooden toothpick in half and tie a piece of thread or ribbon to the larger half. Knot it securely and then insert the toothpick into the blown egg. Hang it by the thread sticking out of the hole.

Gift Ideas

Surprise Eggs

These eggs will be a special treat in your children's Easter baskets; or, make them with your children as gifts for their friends and neighbors.

Enlarge the hole in one end of a blown egg to 1/2" in diameter. Clean the inside thoroughly. Dye and decorate the shell as desired. You might want to put the recipient's name on the egg. When dry, fill the egg and cover the hole with an Easter sticker. Some nice surprises to put in your egg are:

- An Easter story
- The story of the first Easter
- A poem written on a narrow roll of paper and tied with a string
- A special note of love and appreciation
- A thank-you note for a job well done
- An invitation to a dinner or a part
- A note announcing a gift of service you are giving to the person
- Small wrapped candies
- A tiny gift, such as jewelry, tickets to an event, money, etc.

Letters From the Easter Bunny

The Easter Bunny can leave notes and letters for the believing children. He can tell them about his family and their various adventures in making and delivering eggs.

Family Activities

Egg Decorating

One of the joys of Easter is the traditional egg-decorating session. As you decorate, discuss how the egg can be an emblem of the resurrection. An egg appears lifeless, but out of it comes new life. The egg is compared to the tomb. The chick is entombed, and when the time is right, comes to life. So will the dead rise from their graves.

Sticker Eggs

Dye the eggs. When they're dry, decorate them with Easter stickers or dots or other shapes (available at craft supply stores).

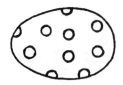

Resist Eggs

Dye the eggs a light color, or leave them white. Stick adhesive dots or stars on them, or apply squares in a pattern. If you want lines, apply narrow strips of masking tape. Then dip the eggs in a darker color of dye than first used. Let them dry before removing the stickers or tape.

Tie-Dyed Eggs

Wrap the eggs tightly in a cheap colorful fabric that is likely to "run," putting the inked side of the fabric toward the eggs. Secure the fabric with rubber bands as shown. Dip the eggs in warm water, remove the fabric.

Batik Eggs

Dip the eggs in a light dye. Dry them with a soft cloth. Drip beeswax (available at craft stores) or ordinary candle wax onto the egg in any pattern you want. Then dip the eggs in a darker dye. Dry them. To remove the wax, heat the eggs in a moderate oven for about two minutes, or heat them over a candle flame until the wax has melted. Wipe the eggs with dry tissue.

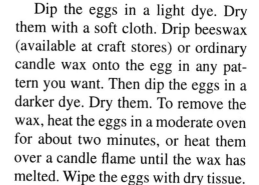

Leaf Printed Eggs

Dye the eggs, if desired, and let them dry. Press a small leaf or leaves against them. Secure the leaves in place by wrapping the eggs tightly in pieces of cheesecloth or nylon stocking. Tie the tops of the cloth tightly with a rubber band. Dip the eggs in a different-colored dye. Rest them on a piece of crumpled foil until the cloth is dry, then remove the cloth to see your patterns.

Yarn Eggs

Start in center of an egg by brushing it with white glue. Then wrap yarn around it. Continue gluing and wrapping, pushing the rows tightly together. Glue all the ends carefully to prevent them from coming undone.

Paper-Collage Eggs

Mix equal amounts of white glue and water. Brush the mixture lightly on the eggs. Then overlap torn pieces of colored tissue on eggs, adding glue as necessary.

Family Games

The Egg Hunt

The traditional egg hunt can take many forms. You can hide the eggs inside or outside. They can be hard boiled, chocolate, colored or paper eggs that are exchanged for real ones when the hunt is over. Using paper eggs eliminates the problem of eggs spoiling when they're not found. Some families hide an equal number of different-colored eggs and assign each child a color to prevent one child from getting more than the others.

Easter Treasure Hunt

Write clues on hard boiled eggs. Give the first egg to the treasure hunters and it will lead them to the second egg, and so on until the last egg leads them to the treasure.

Egg Rolling

This is another very old Easter tradition that was brought to the United States from England. Every year an egg roll is held on the White House lawn. You can have your own on any hillside. Each person needs several hard boiled eggs. Everyone lines up a yard or so apart and rolls their egg down the hill. The egg that rolls the farthest without cracking wins. Even the smallest crack disqualifies an egg.

Egg Tapping

If you're a competitive family, you will enjoy this old game. Two players begin by facing each other, holding a hard cooked egg so that just the small end shows. They tap the ends of their eggs together. This continues until one egg cracks. The winner then goes on to challenge the next player and so on until everyone has played and the "Champion Egg Tapper" has been found.

Egg Toss

This traditional Easter activity is often played with raw eggs. Water balloons are suggested for the fainthearted! Fill small balloons half full of water and tie a knot to hold the water in. Divide the players into pairs and line them up facing each other, about three feet apart. On the count of three, everyone tosses their egg or balloon to their partner, who attempts to catch it without breaking it. Everyone then takes one step backwards and the eggs or balloons are tossed back. When one breaks, that couple is out. Play continues until only the winning couple remains.

Food Fun

Bunny Biscuits for Easter Breakfast

To delight little children and increase their fun, let them help make these for the family.

1. Roll out your favorite biscuit dough. You might want to double your recipe as it takes two biscuits to make each bunny.
2. Cut the dough into circles. Cut half of the circles in half.
3. Place the two halves on sheet in a v, as shown, for ears.
4. Moisten the lower edges of the ears and top them with a round biscuit, pressing the edges together.
5. Brush the completed bunnies with melted butter and sprinkle them with cinnamon sugar.
6. Bake and cool them on a rack. (Remove them very carefully.)
7. When cool, decorate them with frosting, or with candies stuck on with frosting. Licorice whiskers can be added.

Shredded-Wheat Easter Nests

This is an ideal recipe for small cooks—their nests look so natural. Set one at each person's place at the table for breakfast, lunch, or dinner.

1. Melt 1/4 cup of butter in a saucepan.
2. Add and melt 40 large marshmallows, stirring constantly.
3. Remove from heat and stir in 5 cups of crumbled shredded wheat.

4. Allow mixture to cool a minute or two, then butter your hands and shape the Shredded Wheat into nests. Fill them with colored eggs while still warm.

Sugar-Cookie Eggs

For a family activity, decorate a whole basketful of beautiful sugar-cookie eggs and take them to someone who needs a lift. Remember the rule: any that aren't perfect can be eaten!
1. Mix your favorite sugar-cookie dough.
2. Make an egg-shaped cookie cutter from a clean tin can: simply remove both ends of the can and squeeze the two sides together until you have a perfect egg shape.
3. Roll out the dough and cut it into egg shapes. Bake it as directed.
4. When the cookies are cooled, make butter-cream icing tinted with various pastel colors.
5. Line the bowls of colored icing down the middle of the table. Set out lots of sprinkles and different kinds of decorations, the more the better. Then let your crew go to work!

Easter-Basket Cakes

These charming cakes will be family favorites. Visit the craft store for cute Easter bunnies and chicks to put in your cake baskets (Ones on picks are handy.) Buy narrow ribbons in Easter colors too.
1. Cut rounds from a sheet cake using a large can for a cutter.
2. Stack 2 or 3, adding frosting between the layers to hold them together.
3. Set each basket cake on a foil-covered cardboard circle. Hollow out the top layer to form a basket. Leave a 3/4" border around the basket opening to insert a handle.
4. Frost the entire basket except for the inside. Immediately, sprinkle it with pastel-tinted flaked coconut. To tint the coconut, place it in a jar and add a few drops of food coloring. Screw on the lid and shake it until all the coconut is coated.
5. Fill the basket with small candy eggs, bunnies, chicks, etc.

6. Make a basket handle by braiding or twining several colors of ribbon around the middle section of a pipe cleaner (leave the ends of pipe cleaner free to insert into the cake). Knot the ends of the ribbon and tie it in bows.

Variation: For a large Easter basket, hollow out one 9" layer cake and follow the above directions except for the handle. Make the handle from a wire coat hanger. Cover it with aluminum foil, then wrap it with ribbon.

16
July Fourth,
Independence Day

The biggest birthday party of the year is July 4th! Enjoy the parades, picnics, ball games, family reunions and fireworks, but don't forget the reason for the celebration. Develop some traditions with your family that pass on a love for your country and the freedom you enjoy to the next generation.

Fourth-of-July Speech

In many communities, before the advent of radio and television, the fourth of July was an occasion that required a speech. It was a great honor to be asked to give your town's Fourth-of-July oration. A two-hour speech was the minimum requirement! Revive this tradition in your family by calling on a member of the family to give a Fourth-of-July speech each year. Please shorten the time requirement to about two minutes. Make it an honor in your family to be the one asked to give the speech.

Wear the Colors

Make it a tradition to only wear red, white and blue on the fourth of July. This small tradition will be a favorite for younger children, who will also proudly wear any outfit you make or buy for them.

Birthday Cake

What's a birthday without a cake? Make it a tradition to always bake a cake for the Fourth. Assign the job to a different family member each year and see all the creative ways they will come up with to honor their country. Besides the traditional flag cake, try one shaped and frosted to look like the Declaration of Independence, the Statue of Liberty, John Hancock's famous signature, the Liberty Bell, or the five committee members named to draft the declaration.

Name the States

Hand out pens and papers and see who can name all the states. Set a time limit. If that seems too easy for some members of your family, require them to write the state capitals as well. Make the game a tradition and you'll be surprised how it will motivate the family to learn these!

What's Your Patriotic I.Q.?

Have a member of the family make up a short quiz to test everyone's knowledge of their county's beginning. You can make all the questions serious or you can include a few fun questions, such as:

Q: Where was the Declaration of Independence signed?

A: On the bottom!

The National Anthem

Give everyone a copy of the Star Spangled Banner with 10-15 words left blank. See who can fill in the blanks correctly. Move on to other verses or anthems. Those family members who cannot put in all the words must struggle through the first verse out loud for the family's enjoyment.

Skits, Plays, and Pageants

Children are natural actors and most of them love nothing better than to put on a show. Re-enact some of the events to do with the first Independence Day. This will take a little homework. Re-enact the moment when John Hancock affixed his signature to the Declaration of Independence (don't forget the feather pen), the Boston Tea Party, or the Battle of Concord.

Visit an Historic Site

Plan a trip to an historic site. Enjoy a picnic afterward.

Fourth-of-July Picnic

After the parade, spread out the picnic. Decorate with red, white, and blue. Serve a few dishes that reflect the color scheme as well. Use flags, stars, liberty bells, streamers and firecrackers. Here are a few foods the whole family can get involved in preparing.

Super Sandwich

Make a 6-foot-long sandwich for your July 4th picnic. It can be carried on a 1" x 10" board that is wrapped in foil. Cut the ends off long loaves of French bread and place the loaves together end to end. Slice the top off, but not all the way through. Tear out some bread to form a depression. Fill it generously with all your favorite fillings.

Firecracker Cakes

Buy chocolate-covered jelly roll cakes, or make your own jelly rolls and cut them in 4 1/2" lengths. Stand them up to resemble firecrackers. Pipe "July 4th" on the front of each and a coil of icing on the top. Insert a red candle in the center of the coil for a fuse. Light them up.

Star-Shaped Cookies

Make 50 star-shaped cookies, and pipe the names of each state on with icing. Serve them on red and white paper-covered cardboard.

17

Halloween

The sights and sounds of little ghosts and goblins running down the sidewalks, jack o' lanterns burning brightly on every doorstep, and eerie music wafting down the block (pierced by the occasional scream) spell Halloween in our neighborhood. The drama and excitement of this holiday offer many possibilities for family fun. Because of concern for our children's safety, parental involvement in Halloween celebrations has become a necessity. That said, let's conjure up some Halloween fun for the entire family!

Pumpkin Growing and Carving

An adult should always supervise or actually do the cutting rather than young children. However, young children can draw the cutting lines and take out all the "insides," which is their favorite part anyway. Instead of cutting faces out with knives, you also can paint faces on with felt-tip pens or pumpkin-face appliques.

Roasted Pumpkin Seeds

A tradition at our house is to save some of the pumpkin seeds and roast them. Here is how you do it:
1. Wash the seeds in a strainer to get all the pulp and strings off.
2. Gently boil the seeds in a pot of salted water for about 10 minutes.
3. Dry them on a towel.
4. Mix together in a bowl:
      4 cups of seeds
      2 tsp. salt

2 tsp. Worcestershire sauce

6 T. melted butter

5. Spread the seeds out thinly a on cookie sheet and bake at 225 degrees for an hour or more, stirring occasionally. Cook them until they're crisp and delicious.

Preparing for the Trick-or-Treaters

Greeting the little trick-or-treaters is a highlight of Halloween. In our neighborhood, several families give more than treats—they give a Halloween theatrical experience that includes everything that makes Halloween fun! Greet the little hob-goblins as a gypsy and tell a fortune or two. Be a witch stirring a black brew and give out small drinks to children you know. Team up with another member of the family and dress as a couple—Frankenstein and his bride, Laurel and Hardy, two jailbirds chained together. Older children who secretly wish they could be out trick-or-treating will enjoy getting into the theatrics of the night.

Creating the Right Atmosphere

Remember, this is theatre. Try to create a Halloween atmosphere, especially at your doorway, but keep your audience in mind. You don't want to frighten them away, right?

Crepe Paper

Crepe paper streamers (black and purple) that have been crumpled up to look ragged can appear spooky, especially in a breeze.

Stuffed Man

The stuffed man is a tradition that keeps them guessing. Simply stuff a long-sleeved shirt, pants, socks, gloves and a section of pantyhose for a head. Hold everything together with safety pins or long stitches. Dress him as a vampire or some other monster after he's completed. Sit him in your doorway, on the front porch, or behind a tree. If desired, let someone dress the same way, with a cloth over his face, gloves and stuffing in his clothes for an "unrealistic" look. Have him sit motionless next to the fake one until the trick-or-treaters have their treats. Then let him "surprise" them!

Tree Ghosts

Every Halloween I see one of my neighbors and her little children hanging one of these on her bushes. Make the ghost's head by crumpling up a wad of newspapers. Tie a square of sheeting or a white kitchen garbage bag around it. Hang the ghost by the top of its head and let it blow in the wind.

Floating Specter

Every haunted house needs a Specter or two. Blow up a white balloon and suspend it with a long black thread. Draw a face with a waterproof felt marker. Tie wisps of crinkled tissue paper "hair" around the neck of the balloon. Tape a white nylon scarf body on. Turn out the lights and shine a flashlight or spotlight on your Specter to give people a start. Try him in your doorway or a window.

Dry Ice Jack o' Lantern

Let all the trick-or-treaters that come to your door be greeted with this eerie jack o' lantern. You will need:

- an extra-large pumpkin
- a gallon tin can
- box of salt
- dry ice (get it from a supermarket or ice cream store)
- small flashlight
- heavy gloves

1. Clean out the pumpkin and carve a face in it. Place the can inside the pumpkin. Insert the flashlight between the can and the pumpkin wall.
2. Fill the can 3/4 full of *hot* water and add 1/2 cup of salt. Mix.
3. *Wear gloves* as you drop in two or three pieces of dry ice to get your pumpkin steaming. As necessary, add more every 15-20 minutes or when the bubbling stops. Use tongs or a slotted spoon to remove any remaining ice, empty the water can and refill it with hot water, salt and more ice. (*Caution:* Extreme care must be taken with dry ice. Always wear gloves and keep it out of children's reach. Use it only in a ventilated area!)

A Halloween Dinner

Have a holiday dinner for your family and friends during the Halloween week. Let the whole family prepare the table decorations and food, or take one child aside and the two of you can surprise the others. (This is a good opportunity for spending some one-on-one time.) Here are some ideas to help make your dinner a success.

Jack o' Lantern Favor

Kids can make these cute favors. Wrap an apple, orange or popcorn ball (most children prefer the popcorn ball!) in plastic wrap and then in orange crepe paper. Tie it at the top with thick green yarn. Draw on a face with a black permanent marker.

Orange Pumpkin Dinner Favor or Salad

Cut tops off extra-large oranges and clean the flesh out. Carve a jack o' lantern face on the side. Line with plastic wrap if desired and fill it with candies. Cut a tiny hole in the top (lid) of the orange and insert a cinnamon stick for a "pumpkin" stem.

Variation: fill the orange with slightly thickened jello salad and chill it in the refrigerator until set.

Pumpkin Brew

Serve a Halloween drink in a large, hollowed-out, chilled pumpkin. Line it with plastic wrap and pour in the beverage just before serving. Use a punch ladle for serving and float plastic spiders and bugs in it. This can be your table centerpiece.

Variation: Fill your hollowed-out pumpkin with treats or cookies for your dessert. Have them spilling out the top. Tuck in a few Halloween decorations to complete your arrangement.

Orange Halloween Punch

Mix in a large bowl with electric mixer:
> 1 qt. vanilla ice cream, softened
> 1 qt. orange sherbet
> 48 oz. can pineapple juice

Just before serving pour in:
> 1 qt. ginger ale

The Great Pumpkin Cookie

1. Mix up your favorite drop cookie dough and bake it in a pizza pan to make one giant cookie. (Spread the dough only the thickness of an ordinary cookie.) Let it cool on a rack.
2. Add a jack o' lantern face with frosting and candies. The face could also be formed of whole pecans or other nuts, M&M's, fruit-flavored jelly slices, gumdrops, etc. If desired, press them into the dough before baking to form the face.

Table Spooks

Dress up your Halloween table with these easy-to-make spooks. Assemble as in the illustration. For a ghost you need each of the following:

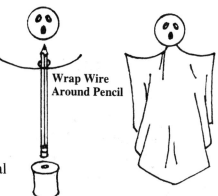

Wrap Wire Around Pencil

- small styrofoam head
- sharp pencil
- regular thread spool
- large white napkin or material
- black yarn
- marker pen
- firm wire

Traditional Halloween Foods for Your Halloween Dinner

Apples	**Pumpkins**
Apple Cider	Pumpkin Bread
Carmel Apples	Pumpkin Cake
Baked Apples	Pumpkin Cookies
Apple Cake	Pumpkin Pie

Dinner in a Pumpkin
(casserole of hamburger,
rice and soup cooked
in a pumpkin)
Pumpkin Soup
(served in a pumpkin)
Pumpkin-shaped Foods
Halloween Hamburgers with
a cheese slice pumpkin
cut-out on top

Pumpkin-wiches (a pumpkin-
shaped cheese slice
on bread)
Popcorn Balls
Gingerbread
Doughnuts
Root Beer
Spook-ghetti
Fortune Cake (with fortune
symbols baked inside)
Nuts

Family Games and Activities

Apple Bobbing

You have to do it, it's a tradition! To add an element of excitement, write fortunes and place one in each apple. Write them on tiny slips of paper and push them into a slit cut in the apple. Dip the slit into warm melted paraffin wax to keep the fortune dry and prevent browning.

Wink Murder

You need at least seven people to have fun playing this game. Pass around a hat containing folded slips of paper, all of which are blank except for one marked with an X. The player who receives the X becomes the murderer. Players sit in a loose circle and converse naturally while the killer goes to work. If he catches a victim's eye and winks at him or her, that person is a goner, but they must count to 15 silently before dying. Deaths can be dramatic, but must be brief!

The object for all players is to catch the murderer before everyone dies. Anyone who believes he has caught the killer in the act must accuse the *victim* before he dies, not the murderer. If right, he can then confront the murderer. If the accuser is wrong in either of his accusations, he must die, and the game continues. The game is over when the murderer is found out.

Pass the Parcel

Prepare the parcel by wrapping a small gift. Continue wrapping it over and over, tucking in little surprises every now and then. Surprises could be plastic spiders and bugs, ghost suckers, Halloween pencils, stickers and treats. Everyone sits in a circle and passes the parcel around as Halloween music is played. When the music stops, whoever is holding the parcel at that precise moment gets to take off one layer of paper to see if he gets a prize. The game continues until the parcel is unwrapped. If you have young children, tuck in lots of surprises so that no one is disappointed.

Gingerbread Haunted House

If you are always too busy at Christmas to make a gingerbread house, consider making one for Halloween. Make it big with lots of windows and place a spook at each one! Make bats, cats, ghosts, goblins, and witches from some of the dough to set at windows, door and in the yard. Decorate with black, brown and orange cookies and candies. Let everyone put their heads together to create something frighteningly good!

18
Thanksgiving

Be careful, or this wonderful day could be viewed by family members as a time to eat and be merry and nothing more. Thanksgiving, when handled properly within the home, gives us an opportunity to pause, count our blessings and express our thanks through words and actions. Every day should be a day of thanksgiving: start by focusing on gratitude during the whole month of November.

Thanksgiving can be the best time to reflect on everything wonderful and good in our lives. There is the sheer beauty of the Thanksgiving table with autumn's bounty and laden with summer's fruits from our storeroom shelves. There is the gathering of families around the table and the security of the harvest home. It is a time to thank God for all of his blessings, and to thank others who have helped us in our lives.

Decorating

For your Thanksgiving decorations, look to the bountiful harvest. Baskets brimming with gourds, dried corn, squash, pumpkins and fruits, shocks of corn, bunches of hanging vegetables, dried flowers and sheaves of wheat, all give us the feeling of a harvest home. Thanksgiving offers a unique appreciation for the beauties of nature. Have your children help make pleasing arrangements.

Growing Gourds

Let your children plant some gourd seeds in the spring for Thanksgiving decorations. Watching them grow and seeing all of the different varieties that emerge provides a lot of entertainment for younger children. They

might even set up a table in the fall and sell them to friends and neighbors. Gourds have a lot of sales appeal among craft-minded people.

Pumpkin Baskets

Make a novel centerpiece for your Thanksgiving table by carving a pumpkin into a basket with handles. Line the inside with plastic wrap and fill it with fruits. Surround with vines, leaves, and pieces of fruit.

Pumpkin Centerpiece

Cut the top off a pumpkin. Place a container of water inside it and fill it with an arrangement of bold autumn flowers.

Family Activities

Thank-You Notes

Gratitude is a learned trait. We can train ourselves and our children to be grateful, but unexpressed thoughts of gratitude are no more useful than seeds given to a starving man. Imagine the good that could be done if all our feelings of thankfulness were expressed so that they could grow and blossom, bringing forth fruit in the lives of those around us.

Ask family members to make a list of people who they have been grateful for during the last year. Share your list and ask everyone to write notes of gratitude to at least two people.

At this time of the year send thank you cards to anyone who has made a difference in your life: the school bus driver, the postman, your hairdresser, etc. Being liberal with words of gratitude and praise is a good tradition!

Thanksgiving Baskets

Before you sit down to your Thanksgiving feast, pause to think about what others will be eating. Will their tables be as laden as yours? If you have been abundantly blessed, consider starting a Thanksgiving basket tradition. Fill a basket (or more) for someone in need and challenge everyone in the family to buy one item for the basket. Deliver it anonymously from "a friend."

Thanksgiving Mural

The first Thanksgiving was celebrated in October, 1621 by pilgrims who gathered to give thanks to God for their first harvest. They were joined by friendly Indians, and the planned one-day religious celebration became a three-day party with games and sports. Get out a large piece of butcher paper, markers, paints and crayons and let the whole family contribute to a giant mural depicting the first Thanksgiving.

Variation: Is a member of your family away at college or elsewhere? Why not lay an eight-foot roll of paper out on the floor and have everyone stake their claim. Make a giant mural for her, just to let her know you are thankful for her and miss her.

Bartering Game

This game helps children learn how the Indians and the Pilgrims bartered with each other to obtain items they needed. Wrap up gifts of different shapes and sizes, one for each person. Distribute the gifts and let everyone shake his package without opening it. If a person doesn't wish to keep his gift, he must barter with someone else to exchange it. Allow 5 or 6 minutes to complete all the trades. (This can also be fun for Family Home Evening treats—wrap up different treats and barter!)

Turkey Talk

If you're having a big crowd for Thanksgiving, this game can be fun. As guests arrive, pin a paper turkey to their shirts. Explain that turkeys can be won or lost and that a prize will be awarded to the person who has collected the most turkeys before dinner time. To win a turkey you must get someone to say "no" by asking a question, or by any other devious method possible!

Giving Thanks

Before beginning the Thanksgiving feast, go around the table and have the participants express something for which they are thankful.

Who's Thankful For . . .

While you're sitting around the Thanksgiving table, too full to eat another bite, play this little game. Give everyone a pen and a numbered paper and have them write their name and what they are most thankful for this year. Take the papers in and give everyone a new paper. Read out the number and the reason for thankfulness and ask everyone to write who they think wrote each reason. When all are finished, give the correct answers so people can check their papers. Give a prize to the most perceptive person.

19
Merry Christmas!

"It's the most wonderful time of the year . . . " Surely the world is closer to heaven at this time of year than at any other. If you have been missing the special magic of this season, maybe it's time to make some changes. There is a tendency to *prepare* Christmas and present it to our families rather then letting them *experience* it. We buy, we bake, we make, we wrap it up and give it to our children. Doing this may cheat them of the main pleasure of the season, which is *to give*—and we end up in a state of total exhaustion. What we do with our children during the Christmas season is much more important than what we get for them. The ideas suggested in this chapter will help us to do more with our families and emphasize the true meaning of Christmas.

Counting the Days

Promises: Advent Calendar (for small families)

Give promises instead of gifts in an advent calendar. Make a calendar for each child with a pocket to open each morning during December. Suit the promises to each child, and remember, you have to keep your promises. For example:

I will read you your favorite story today.

You do not have to wash the dishes today.

I will pull you around the block on your toboggan.

Paper-Chain Advent Calendar

Make a paper chain with 24 rings and remove one each day. The shorter the chain, the shorter the wait.

Individual Advent Calendars

Make each child his or her own advent calendar to keep in their room. The calendar themes are chosen from each child's current passion; for example, a joke for each day, a quote from Star Trek, a cartoon you've clipped, an amazing fact, a special thought to do with Christmas.

Advent Gift Swag

This looks glorious and is so much fun! You need:

- 24 small gifts (to suit your children, such as: small candies and trinkets)
- 24 small boxes of various sizes
- gift wrap in various colors and designs
- A lot of red, green, and white, curling ribbon
- 24 self-adhesive gift tags
- a beautiful big bow
1. Prepare 24 small gifts. Decorate each one with a bow from the curling ribbon. Place a numbered sticker (from 1-24) and a family member's name on each gift so you can take turns opening the gifts.

2. Cut 24 long pieces of ribbon to tie to the gifts. Take hold of all the ribbons, adjust the arrangement until it is pleasing (boxes should hang at different lengths), then tie a large knot at the top.
3. Add lots of curling ribbon to fill out the arrangement and attach a large red bow on the top. Hang.

Advent Tree

The Christmas season is a good time to review the life of Christ with your family. Here's an idea that will help you do this in a memorable way.

Set up a small evergreen tree or a swag on your mantle. Each day in December, hang an ornament depicting an event in the life of the Savior or one of his teachings. Children can take turns placing the ornament on the tree. Read the scripture that goes with the ornament and discuss it. By December 25th your family will have reviewed much of the life and teachings of the Savior.

Create the 24 ornaments from wood or paper. Write the corresponding scripture and its number on the back or bottom of each ornament with a permanent marker. Here is a suggested list of ornaments, but feel free to make your own.

Ornament List

1. Angel	Luke 1:26-38
2. Manger	Luke 2:1-19
3. Star	Matthew 2:1-23
4. Temple	Luke 2:40-52
5. Dove	Matthew 3:1-17, Mark 1:1-10
6. Bread	Matthew 4:1-11
7. Candlestick	Matthew 5:1-18
8. Sun	Matthew 5:38-48
9. Treasure Chest	Matthew 6:19-24
10. Mote	Matthew 7:1-5
11. House on Rock	Luke 6:43-49, Matthew 7:21-27
12. Ship	Mark 4:35-41

13. Sheep	Luke 15:3-32
14. Names of the 12 on scroll	Matthew 10
15. Whale	Matthew 12:39-45
16. Baskets with Loaves & Fishes	John 6:1-14
17. Waves	Matthew 14:23-33
18. Key	Matthew 16:13-20
19. Heart	Matthew 15:1-20
20. Commandment Tablets	Matthew 22:36-40
21. Lamp	Matthew 25:1-13
22. Sheep & Goat	Matthew 25:31-46
23. Bread & Cup	Matthew 26:17-29
24. Empty Tomb or Stone	John 20:1-31

Christmas Traditions That Emphasize Service and Love

In an earlier chapter we discussed family service ideas that can last throughout the year. Here are some of them with a Christmas twist!

Santa For the Day

Cut small strips of paper, one for each member of your family. Write "Santa" on one of the slips. Place folded slips in a Christmas container. Each morning, for a week or longer, the slips are drawn. Whoever picks the "Santa" slip is Santa for the day and performs small acts of kindness and giving in secret.

Santa Calling Cards

This adds an element of fun. You will need a package of narrow Christmas gift tags and an envelope for each member of the family. Place

five or six blank gift tags in each envelope except one. In that envelope place five or six gift tags that say "Santa was here." When the envelopes are drawn, whoever receives the Santa calling cards is Santa. When he performs his good deeds he leaves a calling card!

Christmas Angels

This is a variation of the Santa tradition (see above), the advantage being that everyone has an opportunity to serve every day. Family members write their names on slips of paper which are put in a box. Each day everyone draws a name and they become that person's Christmas Angel, performing secret acts of kindness for them. Before beginning the project, discuss ways to give service so that the "angels" will be prepared and can be more creative.

Christmas Pixies

As a family, make a list of people you know that are in need. Prepare gift boxes for them and deliver them anonymously as a family. Or, as pixies, you might shovel their walks, take them a meal, baby sit their children, or visit them. Think of what they need the most and try to fill that need.

Christmas Visits

Christmas is the loneliest time of the year for many people. Give the gifts of time and friendship—no cost involved. Visit the elderly and the sick. Invite widows and widowers to your home for a nice home-cooked meal and a visit. Children can brighten the days of the elderly by popping in for short visits on a regular basis.

Gift-Giving to Add to the Spirit of Christmas

Gifts for the Savior

What can I give Him,
Poor as I am.
If I were a Shepherd
I'd give him a lamb . . .

If I were a Wiseman,
I would do my part.
But what can I give Him?
I can give my heart!

Christmas is the birthday of the Savior. If we all get presents on our birthdays, it follows that we should give the Savior a gift for his birthday. Prepare a small white envelope (see the pattern below) and

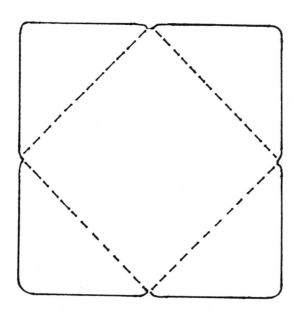

a slip of paper for each member of the family. After a family discussion, have each person privately write what gift he or she would like to give. Hang the little envelopes on the Christmas tree to serve as reminders during the holiday season. When the tree is taken down, hang the envelopes in everyone's bedrooms. After the envelopes are hung, serve a birthday cake for Jesus to end this family activity.

Envelope Pattern for Gifts for the Savior

Instructions:
1. Trace the pattern and cut it out.
2. Trace the envelope using the pattern, and cut it out.
3. Fold on the lines.
4. Use a glue stick to secure the envelope.
5. Punch a hole and hang it with a ribbon or gold cord.

Gifts For Charity

Go shopping as a family and let each family member buy one present. Leave those presents with a charity group that distributes parcels to families in need. If children earn the money for their gifts, it will be much more meaningful to them. Start this project on November 1 to allow time for the money to be earned.

Twelve Days of Christmas Gift Box

Make a special present for someone. Decorate a box and fill it with 12 numbered gifts to be opened on each of the 12 days before Christmas.

Surprise Balls

Brighten someone's day by making a surprise ball for him! Place a small gift on the end of a crepe-paper streamer and begin to wind the streamer around and around the gift. Tuck in little surprises as you go, such as jokes, candies, clues about what is inside and so on.

Keep rolling until you have a ball-shaped gift, them tape up the loose end. These are as much fun to make as they are to receive.

Julkapp Someone

The Julkapp is a Swedish gift-giving tradition that is as fun for the givers as the receivers. To carry out a Julkapp, wrap a present in many layers of paper. The longer it takes to unwrap the gift the better! To deliver your present, knock on the door of a friend's house, open it, throw in the present and run away. The Julkapp comes from a gentler age when people did not have to keep their doors locked!

Julgranskaramell

Hide these tiny presents on your Christmas tree for each member of the family. They do not get to open them until the tree is taken down! This Swedish tradition spreads the fun of Christmas throughout the season.

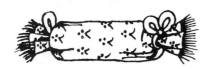

1. Fill empty toilet tissue rolls with candy and/or small toys and wrap them in brightly colored tissue paper.
2. Tie the ends with yarn and fringe them with scissors.

Personalized Gift Stockings

Give a stocking full of tiny gifts. Making and decorating the stocking can be half the fun. Choose a theme for the stocking by thinking about the recipient's personality, interests and favorite sayings.

Examples:

   Cook's Stocking: use kitchen print, write her specialties
   Sewer's Stocking: cover stocking with buttons
   Sport Lover's Stocking: write names of teams, goals scored, etc.
   Teenager's Stocking: write all their favorite sayings
   Missionary's Stocking: map of their mission, cities they served in, names of companions, etc.

Nativity Book

The highlight of one Christmas, when we had a son in the mission field, was making a nativity book for him. We dressed in nativity costumes and took pictures of the nativity story as it unfolded, scene by scene. The hills around our town provided a perfect setting. We even found a donkey and some sheep. The pictures were assembled into a nativity book bound together with ribbons. Under each picture the corresponding scripture verses were written. The borders of each page were decorated with holly leaves. It is a gift that will be in my son's family for generations.

Christmas Experiences

Christmas in Other Lands

Does you family get tired of the same old Christmas traditions? Try celebrating Christmas with traditions from another country. Have a Mexican Christmas party complete with Las Posadas and a pinata. Serve oysters or goose for a French Christmas dinner and put your empty shoes on the doorstep or by the fireplace for Le Petit Noel (the Christ Child) or Pere Noel (Father Christmas) to fill. Get books from the library on Christmas customs in other countries and plan your celebration.

A Christmas Play or Video

Putting on a family play can be a lot of fun! Make up your own version of The Night Before Christmas or the night Christ was born.

Put it on video and show it to extended family for Christmas entertainment.

A Nativity Play

Many families read or act out the nativity story on Christmas Eve. Some have even invested time and money into sewing beautiful nativity costumes. Down through the years these costumes become family heirlooms. The importance attached to the nativity play has helped transmit cherished family values to the children and grandchildren of these families.

Cookie Christmas Cards & Gift Tag

Have a creative and fun-filled baking session for the entire family.
1. Mix your favorite rolled cookie dough that handles easily and is not fragile.
2. For each card, cut a large square of aluminum foil and dust it lightly with flour. Roll 1 cup of dough until it is about 1/4" thick.
3. Place a paper pattern on the dough and cut around it with a sharp knife. Remove the excess dough. Make a small hole or two with a drinking straw where a ribbon will be added later.

4. Lift the foil square onto a cookie sheet and bake. Remove the foil sheet and cool it on wire racks. Do not attempt to remove the cookie from the foil until it is thoroughly cooled. Reopen holes the for ribbons while warm.

5. While waiting for the cookies to cool, use cookie cutters to cut out holly leaves, candy canes, gingerbread men, etc., to decorate your big cookie cards and to make cookie gift tags. Bake and cool them.
6. To decorate, attach cookies to the cards with dabs of frosting. Add candies and cake decorations. Write greetings with frosting. Add a bow.

Christmas Memories Album

Make a fabric-covered Christmas album from a 3-ring binder. Fill it with journal pages and photo sleeves. Every Christmas, record how you celebrated, what special gifts were given and received, the Christmas menu, etc. Have each family member share his or her favorite Christmas memory of the year. Include Christmas photos and mementoes such as children's school art work, cards, and perhaps even a sales flier showing the hottest-selling toy of the year. Pack the album away with the ornaments.

Twelve Days-of-Christmas Countdown

Expand the joy of Christmas to include a special activity for each of the twelve days before Christmas. Plan carefully to be sure you can follow through on these commitments. Make a calendar with sealed doors, or write each activity on a card. Seal the cards in tiny boxes and giftwrap them. Number the boxes from 1-12 and arrange them on a shelf, or hang them from a big bow. Some ideas for the activities are:

Kids choose the supper menu
Midnight Madness (party until midnight)
Go to a Christmas movie together
No chores for anyone under 20 day
Watch "White Christmas" and eat fudge
Parents pull kids on a toboggan after dark

NOTES

NOTES